Eyewitness Accounts of the American Revolution

Narrative of
Jonathan Rathbun

The New York Times & Arno Press

Reprint Edition 1971 by Arno Press Inc.

*

LC# 76-140878
ISBN 0-405-01217-9

*

Eyewitness Accounts of the American Revolution, Series III
ISBN for complete set: 0-405-01187-3

*

Manufactured in the United States of America

THE NARRATIVE OF

JONATHAN RATHBUN

OF THE CAPTURE OF FORT GRISWOLD, THE MASSACRE THAT
FOLLOWED, AND THE BURNING OF NEW LONDON,
CONN., SEPTEMBER 6, 1781.

WITH THE NARRATIVES OF RUFUS AVERY
AND STEPHEN HEMPSTEAD,
EYE WITNESSES.

NEW LONDON, CONN.
1840

NEW AND REVISED EDITION, INCLUDING THE NARRATIVE
OF THOMAS HERTTELL, 1832.

NEW YORK
Reprinted
WILLIAM ABBATT
1911
(Being Extra No. 15 of THE MAGAZINE OF HISTORY WITH NOTES AND QUERIES.)

NARRATIVE

OF

JONATHAN RATHBUN,

WITH

ACCURATE ACCOUNTS

OF THE

CAPTURE OF GROTON FORT,

THE

MASSACRE THAT FOLLOWED,

AND THE

SACKING AND BURNING OF NEW LONDON,

September **6, 1781,** *by the British Forces, under the command of the*

TRAITOR BENEDICT ARNOLD.

———

BY RUFUS AVERY

AND

STEPHEN HEMPSTEAD,

Eye witnesses of the same.

———

TOGETHER WITH AN

INTERESTING APPENDIX.

EDITOR'S PREFACE

Personal narratives of private soldiers of our Revolution are invaluable, though as short as they are few in number (not a dozen in all are known to the writer).

This little volume, which bears no place of publication, was probably published at New London. It includes the names of the killed and wounded at the capture of Fort Griswold, and we have added the account of Thomas Herttell, taken from the New York *Sun* of —, 1832 (it has only once appeared in book form, and that many years ago).

As Rathbun has been accused of "doctoring" Avery's narrative, we print the latter's account, after Rathbun's version, taken from what is said to have been the only copy made from the original MS. Yet we find even in this some variations. Rathbun probably thought a more "hifalutin" style would help the sale of his book.

ORIGINAL PREFACE

Whoever reads the Narratives which follow, will feel himself indebted to Mr. Rathbun, the proprietor of the work, for the indefatigable industry, with which, for several years, he has employed himself in collecting the materials. When more than seventy years of age, he found himself in poverty; and as a measure of relief he conceived the plan of this publication, which he has now the happiness of presenting to the patronage of a discerning public. He has often been forced by the necessities which a destitute old age, infirm health and a sick family imposed on him, to solicit the charities of the beneficent for his relief. Now he has the pleasing consciousness of offering to his fellow citizens a work which will no doubt nurture the spirit of patriotism wherever it may be circulated; while the moderate profits which he anticipates will relieve, at least to a good degree, the wants of his old age. He justly feels, in the opinion of the writer of this Preface, that his patrons will find themselves doubly repaid by the value of his book, and at the same time experience the satisfaction of saving one of the last soldiers of the American Revolution from the pain of begging his daily bread. The Narrative of Mr. Rathbun, with which the volume opens, will still further disclose the claims which he has on the patronage of all who value the blessing of a free government.

The Narrative of Mr. Avery has never before been given to the public, and will be found to contain the most interesting incidents of the capture of Groton Fort, expressed in the descriptive and glowing language of an eye witness.

The other articles need only be read to be highly appreciated. They are thought to add much to the value of the work.

The whole presents to the public a connected view of many

minute particulars respecting the events of the fatal 6th of September, 1781, which have never before appeared in print; and though history has recorded the outlines and monuments stand to perpetuate the sanguinary facts, those who read this account will have an impression of that day which none but an actor in the scene can impart.

Fathers, read it to your children, and early impress on their minds a love for Freedom, and teach them to detest a traitor like Arnold, and to scorn the inhuman and dishonorable conduct of the frenzied villain who murdered our brave Ledyard with his own sword after surrendering!

For the perusal of the young, it is especially appropriate, as what they can obtain from history will be explained to their understandings, and when those in the vicinity tread the ground of New London and Groton, they will feel as if a voice echoed from the now peaceful hills, inspiring them with new ardour and zeal for their rights as freemen, and boldness in defending their country from foreign invasion.

NARRATIVE OF JONATHAN RATHBUN

I WAS born in Colchester, Connecticut, in 1765. When sixteen years of age, I joined as a volunteer a company of militia, belonging to my native town, and marched to the relief of New London, intelligence having just reached us of an attack on that place by the British, under the conduct of the traitor Benedict Arnold. We left home to the number of about one hundred men, early in the morning of the 7th of September, 1781, the day after the battle. On our arrival in New London we witnessed a scene of suffering and horror which surpasses description. The enemy were not to be found, but they had left behind them the marks of their barbarism and cruelty. The city was in ashes. More than one hundred and thirty naked chimneys were standing in the midst of the smoking ruins of stores and dwelling houses. Very little property had escaped the conflagration except a part of the shipping, which on the first alarm was sent up the river. But though the city was destroyed it was far from being deserted. Numerous companies of militia from the neighborhood were pouring into the town; and the inhabitants, who had fled from their burning dwellings, were returning to gaze with anguish on the worthless remains of their property. Women were seen walking with consternation and despair depicted in their countenances, leading or carrying in their arms their fatherless and houseless babes, who in a few short hours had been bereaved of all that was dear on earth. Their homes, their provisions, and even their apparel were the spoils of the enemy or lay in ashes at their feet. Some were inquiring with the deepest distress for the mangled bodies of their friends, while others were seen following the carts which bore their murdered fathers, husbands or brothers to the grave. More than forty widows were made on that fatal day. Never can I forget the tears, the sobs, the shrieks of woe which fell from the kindred of our brave countrymen, who then gave their lives to achieve our national independence. It was my melancholy duty to assist in the burial of the dead, which brought me directly into the midst of these heart-rending scenes where the wife first recognized her husband, the mother her son, the sister her brother, in the body of a mangled soldier so disfigured with wounds and clotted with blood and dust, as to be scarcely known! Often on my visits to New London have I walked near the spot where I helped to inter my slaughtered countrymen; and though many years have since rolled away the recollection is still fresh in my mind, awakening anew the strong feelings of sympathy I then felt, and rousing into activity the love of my country.

I recollect several interesting facts, connected with the capture of Fort Griswold and the burning of New London, which, I believe, are not mentioned in the narratives of Messrs. Avery and Hempstead.

After the capture of the fort and the massacre which followed, the enemy laid a line of powder from the magazine of the fort to the sea, intending to blow up the fort, and complete the destruction of the wounded within and around it. Stillman Hotman, who lay not far distant, wounded by three strokes of the bayonet in his body, proposed to a wounded man near him to crawl to this line and saturate the powder with their blood, and thus save the magazine and fort, and perhaps the lives of some of their comrades, not mortally wounded. He alone succeeded in reaching the line, where he was found dead lying on the powder which was completely wet with his blood. I do not find his name among the killed in the list of Mr. Avery.

Another fact of a different character was currently reported at the time and deserves to be recorded to the deeper disgrace of the infamous Arnold. He had a sister living in New London, with whom he dined on the day of the battle, and whose house was set fire to, as is supposed, by his orders, immediately afterwards. Perhaps he found her too much of a patriot for his taste and took this step in revenge.

The next year, 1782, I was led by the spirit which the scenes I had witnessed in New London had fanned into a flame, to leave my father's house and the peaceful pursuits of agriculture, and to enlist as a private in the Connecticut State troops. Never shall I forget the impressive circumstances under which I took the soldier's oath. With five others of my townsmen, who enlisted with me, I was marched into the meeting house on the first Monday in April, it being freeman's day, and there in the presence of a large concourse of people, we swore to discharge our duty faithfully. We were ordered to Fort Stanwich, in Stamford, Connecticut, where I remained during all but the last month of my term of service. Here I was subjected to the usual hardships of a military life. Many a time have I been out for several days on scouting parties, sometimes to the distance of twenty-five miles. These were not only attended with fatigue, cold and hunger, but with no little peril of life. On one occasion a rifle ball passed through my hat and cut away the hair of my head, but a kind Providence protected me.

A party of fourteen men, under Lewis Smith, were surprised by a body of mounted troops to the number of sixty, by whom they were ordered to surrender. Lewis Smith perceiving the hopelessness of resistance against such an overwhelming force, inquired of the British officer in command, whether if they should surrender, they would be treated as prisoners of war. The answer was, yes; but no sooner had they lowered their muskets, than the enemy shot them down.

As a specimen of the hardships to which the private soldier in time of war is constantly liable, I may mention the following.

One evening the orderly sergeants passed around among the men and with a whisper commanded us to equip ourselves without noise; and then we were marched out of the fort to a woods two miles distant, and ordered to lie down on the frozen ground, where we passed a bitter cold night with only a single blanket and our overcoats to protect us. We afterwards learned that this step was taken to avoid the enemy, who it was reported were that night to attack the fort with an overwhelming force. From such exposures and hardships as these my constitution received a shock, from which I have never recovered. The sickness of my father was considered a sufficient reason for giving me a discharge; and after eleven months' service I left Stamford for Colchester. On reaching home I was immediately taken sick, and for six months was unable to do any business. From that time mingled mercies and misfortunes have attended me. The infirmities thus contracted in the service of my country disabled me from arduous manual labor, and much of my life has therefore been spent in trade and other light employments. My heaviest misfortune, however, has been the sickness of my excellent wife, who for forty years has been confined to her bed, and for whose medication and comfort, with the other expenses of my family, the earnings of my industry have proved insufficient, especially since the infirmities of old age have come upon me. But of none of these things do I complain. They are wisely appointed, and have been greatly alleviated by the kindness of a generous community. I mention them for the sole object of interesting my countrymen in my present effort to supply my wants through this little book.

JONATHAN RATHBUN.

NARRATIVE OF RUFUS AVERY

CONTAINING AN ACCOUNT OF THE TRANSACTIONS AT NEW LONDON
AND GROTON, ON THE 6TH SEPTEMBER, 1781, IN HIS OWN WORDS

I HAD charge of the garrison the night previous to the attack. The enemy had not yet appeared near us, nor did we expect them at this time more than ever; but it is true "we know not what shall be on the morrow." About three o'clock in the morning, as soon as daylight appeared, so as I could look off, I saw the fleet in the harbor, a little distance below the light-house; it consisted of thirty-two in number, ships, brigs, schooners and sloops. It may well be imagined that a shock of consternation, and a thrill of dread apprehension flashed over me. I immediately sent for Captain William Latham, who was captain of said fort, and who was near by. He came and saw the fleet, and sent notice to Colonel Ledyard, who was commander of the harbor, and also of Forts Griswold and Trumbull. He ordered two large guns to be loaded with heavy charges of good powder, &c. Captain William Latham took charge of the one which was to be discharged from the northeast part of the fort, and I had to attend the other, on the west side, and thus we as speedily as possible prepared to give alarm to the vicinity, as was to be expected in case of danger, two guns being the specified signal for alarm in distress. But a difficulty now arose from having all our plans communicated by a traitor! The enemy understood our signal was two regular guns, and they fired a third, which broke our alarm, and caused it to signify good news or a prize, and thus it was understood by our troops, and several companies which were lying back ready to come to our assistance in case of necessity were by this measure deterred from coming. The reader may well suppose, though time would not permit us to consider, or anticipate long, yet the sense of our helplessness without additional strength and arms, was dreadful; but the trying events of the few coming hours we had not known! Colonel Ledyard now sent expresses from both forts, to call on every militia captain to hurry with their companies to the forts. But few came: their excuse was that it was but a false alarm, or for some trifling alarm. The enemy's boats now approached and landed eight hundred officers and men, some horses, carriages and cannon, on the Groton side of the river, about eight o'clock in the morning; and another division on the New London side, below the light-house, consisting of about seven hundred officers and men. The army on [the] Groton bank was divided into two divisions. Colonel Ayres[1] took command of the division southeast of the forts, consisting of about half, sheltering them behind a ledge of rocks about one hundred and thirty rods back. Major Montgomery with his division about one hundred and fifty rods from the fort, behind a high hill. The army on New London side of the river, had better and more accommodating land to march on than that on Groton side. As soon as their army had got opposite Fort Trumbull they divided, and one part proceeded to the city of New London, plundered and set fire to the shipping and buildings, the rest marched down to Fort Trumbull. Captain Adam Shapley, who commanded, seeing that he was likely to be overpowered by the enemy, spiked his cannon and embarked on board the boats which had been prepared for him in case of necessity; but the enemy were so quick upon him that before he and his little handful of men could get out of the reach of their guns, seven men were badly wounded in the boats. The remaining one reached Fort Griswold, where, poor fellows, they met a mortal blow.

Ayres and Montgomery got their army stationed about nine o'clock in the morning. When they appeared in sight, we threw a number of shots among them, but they would immediately contrive to disappear behind their hills. About ten o'clock they sent

[1] Eyre.

a flag of truce to demand the surrender of the fort. When the flag was within about forty rods from the fort, we sent a musket ball in front of them and brought them to a stand. Colonel Ledyard called a council of war, to ascertain the minds of his officers and friends about what was best to be done in this momentous hour, when every moment indicated a bloody and decisive battle. They all agreed in council to send a flag to them. They did so, choosing Captain Elijah Avery, Captain Amos Staunton, and Captain John Williams, who went immediately to meet the British flag and receive their demand, which was to give up the fort to them. The council was then inquired of what was to be done, and the answer returned to the British flag was, that "the fort would not be given up to the British." The flag then returned to their division commanded by Ayres, but soon returned to us again; when about a proper distance our flag met them and attended to their summons, and came back to inform Colonel Ledyard that the enemy declared that "if they were obliged to take it by storm, they should put the Martial Law in full force," that is, "what they did not kill by ball, they should put to death by sword and bayonet!" Colonel Ledyard sent back the decisive answer, that "we should not give up the fort to them, let the consequences be what they would."

While these flags were passing and repassing, we were exchanging shots with the British at Fort Trumbull, as they had got possession of it before the battle commenced in action at Fort Griswold. We could throw our shot into Fort Trumbull without any difficulty, but the British could not cause theirs to enter Fort Griswold, because they could not aim high enough. They had got possession and in use, some of our best pieces and ammunition, which were left in Fort Trumbull when Captain Shapley left it and retreated. About eleven o'clock in the morning, when they perceived what we were about to do, they started with both their divisions, Colonel Ayres advancing with his in solid columns. As soon as they reached the level ground, and in a proper range, we saluted them with an eighteen pounder, then loaded with two bags of grapeshot. Captain Elias H. Halsey was the one who directed the guns, and took aim at the enemy. He had long practiced on board a privateer, and manifested his skill at this time. I was at the gun with others when it was discharged into the British ranks, and it cleared a very wide space in their solid columns. It has been reported, by good authority, that about twenty were killed and wounded by that one discharge of grapeshot. As soon as the column was broken by loss of men and officers, they were seen to scatter and trail arms, coming on with a quick step towards the fort, inclining to the west. We continued firing, but they advanced upon the south and west side of the fort. Colonel Ayres was mortally wounded. Major Montgomery now advanced with his division, coming on in solid columns, bearing around to the north until they got east of the redoubt or battery, which was east of the fort, then marching with a quick step into the battery. Here we sent among them large and repeated charges of grapeshot, which destroyed a number, as we could perceive them thinned and broken. Then they started for the fort, a part of them in platoons, discharging their guns; and some of the officers and men scattering, they came around on the east and north side of the fort. Here Major Montgomery [1] fell, near the northeast part of the fort. We might suppose the loss of their commanders might have dismayed them, but they had proceeded so far and the excitement and determination on slaughter was so great, they could not be prevented. As soon as their army had entirely surrounded the gar-

[1] Montgomery was killed with spears, or boarding pikes, in the hands of Captain Adam Shapley, and the negro Jordan Freeman; and Lambo Latham, the second negro patriot of the day, killed a British officer, and was himself killed, receiving thirty-three bayonet wounds.

There was no "negro pew" in that fort, although there was some praying as well as fighting.—William Anderson, of New London, 1853—(*The Colored Patriots of the Revolution*, by W. C. Nell, 1855.)

In 1805 or 1806, an Irish gentleman came to New London and disinterred Montgomery's skull to re-inter it in the family cemetery in Ireland.

rison, a man attempted to open the gates; but he lost his life in a moment, before he could succeed. There was hard fighting and shocking slaughter, and much blood spilt before another attempt was made to open the gates, which was at this time successful; for our little number, which was only one hundred and fifty-five officers and privates (the most of them volunteers), were by this time overpowered. There was then no block house on the parade as there is now, so that the enemy had every chance to wound and kill every man. When they had overpowered us and driven us from our station at the breastwork into the fort, and Colonel Ledyard saw how few men he had remaining to fight with, he ceased resistance. They all left their posts and went on to the open parade in the fort, where the enemy had a fair opportunity to massacre us, as there were only six of us to an hundred of them! This, this was a moment of indescribable misery! We can fight with good hearts while *hope* and prospects of victory aid us; but, after we have fought and bled and availed nothing, to yield to be massacred by the boasting enemy, "tries men's hearts!" Our ground was drenched with human gore; our wounded and dying could not have any attendance, while each man was almost hopeless of his own preservation; but our country's danger caused the most acute anxiety. Now I saw the enemy mount the parapets like so many madmen, all at once seemingly. They swung their hats around, and then discharged their guns into the fort, and then those who had not fallen by ball, they began to massacre with sword and bayonet. I was on the west side of the fort, with Captain Edward Latham and Mr. C. Latham, standing on the platform, and had a full view of the enemy's conduct. I had then a hole through my clothes by a ball, and a bayonet rent through my coat to my flesh. The enemy approached us, knocked down the two men I mentioned, with the breech of their guns, and I expected had ended their lives, but they did not. By this time that division which had been commanded by Montgomery, now under charge of Bloomfield, unbolted the other gates, marched into the fort and formed into a solid column. I at this moment left my station and went across the parade, towards the south end of the barracks. I noticed Colonel William Ledyard on the parade stepping towards the enemy and Bloomfield,[2] gently raising and lowering his sword as a token of bowing and submission; he was about six feet from them when I turned my eyes off from him, and went up to the door of the barracks and looked at the enemy who were discharging their guns through the windows. It was but a moment that I had turned my eyes from Colonel L. and saw him alive, and now I saw him weltering in his gore! Oh, the hellish spite and madness of a man that will murder a reasonable and noble-hearted officer, in the act of submitting and surrendering! I can assure my countrymen that I felt the thrill of such a horrid deed, more than the honorable and martial-like war of months! We are informed that the wretch who murdered him, exclaimed, as he came near, "Who commands this fort?" Ledyard handsomely replied, "I did, but *you* do now:" at the same moment handing him his sword, which the unfeeling villain buried in his breast! The column continued marching towards the south end of the parade, and I could do no better than to go across the parade before them, amid their fire. They discharged three platoons, as I crossed before them at this time. I believe there were not less than five or six hundred of the British on the parade and in the fort. They killed and wounded every man they possibly could, and it was all done in less than two minutes! I had nothing to expect but to drop with the rest; one mad-looking fellow put his bayonet to my side, swearing "by —— he would skipper me!" I looked him earnestly in the face and eyes, and begged him to have mercy and spare my life! I must say, I believe God prevented him from killing me, for he put his bayonet three times into me, and I seemed to be in his power, as well as Lieutenant Enoch Stanton, who was stabbed to the heart and fell at my feet

[2] The Bromfield or Bloomfield was doubtless Stephen Bromfield of the 40th. In the British Army List, for 1781, he is " Blomfield," and in that for 1732, " Bromfield."

at this time. I think no scene ever exceeded this for *continued* and barbarous massacre after surrender. There were two large doors to the magazine, which made a space wide enough to admit ten men to stand in one rank. There marched up a platoon of ten men just by where I stood, and at once discharged their guns into the magazine among our killed and wounded, and also among those who had escaped uninjured, and as soon as these had fired another platoon was ready, and immediately took their place when they fell back. At this moment Bloomfield came swiftly around the corner of the building, and raising his sword with exceeding quickness, exclaimed, "Stop firing! or you will send us all to *hell* together!" I was very near him when he spoke. He knew there must be much powder deposited and scattered about the magazine, and if they continued throwing in fire we should all be blown up. I think it must before this have been the case, had not the ground and everything been wet with human blood. We trod in blood! We trampled under feet the limbs of our countrymen, our neighbors and dear kindred. Our ears were filled with the groans of the dying, when the more stunning sound of the artillery would give place to the death shrieks. After this they ceased killing and went to stripping, not only the dead, but the wounded and those who were not wounded. They then ordered us all who were able to march, to the N. E. part of the parade, and those who could walk to help those who were wounded so bad as not to go of themselves. Mr. Samuel Edgcomb Jr. and myself were ordered to carry out Ensign Charles Eldridge, who was shot through the knee joints; he was a very large heavy man, and with our fasting and violent exercise of the day we were but ill able to do it, or more than to sustain our own weight; but we had to submit. We with all the prisoners were taken out upon the parade, about two rods from the fort, and ordered to sit down immediately, or they would put their bayonets into us. The battle was now ended. It was about one o'clock in the afternoon, and since the hour of eight in the morning, what a scene of carnage, of anxiety, and of loss had

we experienced.   The enemy now began to take care of their dead
and wounded.[3]   They took off six of the outer doors of the barracks, and with four men at each door, they brought in one man at
a time.   There were twenty-four men thus employed for two
hours, as fast as they could walk.   They deposited them on the
west side of the parade in the fort, where it was the most comfortable place, and screened from the hot sun which was pouring down
upon us, aggravating our wounds and causing many to faint and
die who might have lived with good care.   By my side lay two
most worthy and excellent officers, Captain Youngs Ledyard and
Captain Nathan Moore, in the agonies of death.   Their heads
rested on my thighs, as I sat or lay there.   They had their reason
well and spoke.   They asked for water.   I could give them none,
as I was to be thrust through if I got up.   I asked the enemy,
who were passing by us, to give us some water for my dying
friends and for myself.   As the well was near they granted this
request; but even then I feared they would put something poison
into it, that they might get us out of the way the sooner; and they
had said, repeatedly, that the last of us should die before the sun
set!   Oh, what revenge and inhumanity pervaded their steeled
hearts!   They effected what was threatened in the summons, sent
by the flag in the morning, to Colonel Ledyard, "That those who
were not killed by the musket, should be by the sword," &c.   But
I must think they became tired of human butchery, and so let us

[3] Arnold's report to Clinton shows that the British lost five officers: Lieutenant-Colonel
William Montgomery, 54th regiment; Captain George Craigie, 40th regiment; Lieutenant
Henry Williams Smith, 40th regiment; Ensigns Thomas Hyde and Archibald Willock, 40th
regiment, besides forty-six non-commissioned officers and privates killed and one hundred
and twenty-nine wounded.

In addition, the *Connecticut Gazette* of Sept. 21st, said "Seven or eight dead bodies
floated ashore on Groton Neck, and three elsewhere." This would make the total loss two
hundred and seven and shows Fort Griswold to have been one of the bloodiest of en-
counters of the Revolution, in proportion to the numbers engaged.

The Major "Ayres" referred to so often was Edward, of the 40th regiment. He was
not killed, though badly wounded.

It is worth noticing that the 54th was (or had been) André's regiment; and that
Simcoe may have been present, as he was of the 40th.

live. They kept us on the ground, the garrison charged, till about two hours had been spent in taking care of their men; and then came and ordered every man of us that could walk, to "rise up." Sentries were placed around with guns loaded and bayonets fixed, and orders given that every one who would not, in a moment, obey commands, should be shot dead or run through! I had to leave the two dying men who were resting on me, dropping their heads on the cold and hard ground, giving them one last and pitying look. Oh God, this was hard work. They both died that night. We marched down to the bank of the river so as to be ready to embark on board the British vessels. There were about thirty of us surrounded by sentries. Captain Bloomfield then came and took down the names of the prisoners who were able to march down with us. Where I sat I had a fair view of their movements. They were setting fire to the buildings and bringing the plunder and laying it down near us. The sun was about half an hour high. I can never forget the whole appearance of all about me. New London was in flames! The inhabitants deserted their habitations to save life, which was more highly prized. Above and around us were our unburied dead and our dying friends. None to appeal to for sustenance in our exhausted state but a maddened enemy —not allowed to move a step or make any resistance, but with loss of life—and sitting to see the property of our neighbors consumed by fire, or the spoils of a triumphing enemy!

Reader, but little can be described, while much is felt. There were still remaining, near the fort, a great number of the British who were getting ready to leave. They loaded up our large ammunition wagon that belonged to the fort with the wounded men that could not walk, and about twenty of the enemy drew it from the fort to the brow of the hill which leads down to the river. The declivity is very steep for the distance of thirty rods to the river. As soon as the wagon began to move down the hill, it pressed so hard against them that they found they were unable to hold it back, and jumped away from it as quick as possible, leaving it to thrash along down the hill with great speed, till the shafts struck a large apple tree stump, with a most violent crash, hurting the poor dying and wounded men in it in a most inhuman manner. Some of the wounded fell out and fainted away; then a part of the company where I sat ran and brought the men and the wagon along. They by some means got the prisoners who were wounded badly, into a house [4] near by belonging to Ensign Ebenezer Avery, who was one of the wounded in the wagon. Before the prisoners were brought to the house the soldiers had set fire to it, but others put it out and made use of it for this purpose. Captain Bloomfield paroled, to be left at home here, these wounded prisoners, and took Ebenezer Ledyard, Esq. as hostage for them, to see them forthcoming when called for. Now the boats had come for us who could go on board the fleet. The officer spoke with a doleful and menacing tone, "Come, you rebels, go on board." This was a consummation of all I had seen or endured through the day. This wounded my feelings in a thrilling manner. After all my sufferings and toil, to add the pang of leaving my native land, my wife, my good neighbors, and probably to suffer still more with cold and hunger, for already I had learned that I was with a cruel enemy. But I was in the hands of a higher power—over which no human being could hold superior control—and by God's preservation I am still alive, through all the hardships and dangers of the war, while almost every one about me, who shared the same, has met either a natural or an unnatural death. When we, the prisoners, went down to the shore to the boats they would not bring them near, but kept them off where the water was knee deep to us, obliging us, weak and worn as we were, to wade to them. We were marched down in two ranks, one on each side of the boat. The officer spoke very harshly to us, to "get aboard immediately." They rowed us down to an armed sloop, commanded by one Cap-

[4] The blood stains on the floor of this house were visible up to 1881, as Avery (who died in 1828) enjoined upon his family not to efface them.

tain Thomas, as they called him, a refugee Tory,[5] and he lay with his vessel within the fleet. As soon as we were on board, they hurried us down into the hold of the sloop, where were their fires for cooking, and besides being very hot it was filled with smoke. The hatch-way was closed tight, so that we were near sufiocating for want of air to breathe. We begged them to spare our lives, so they gave us some relief by opening the hatch-way and permitting us to come upon deck, by two or three at a time, but not without sentries watching us with gun and bayonet. We were now extremely exhausted and faint for want of food; when after being on board twenty-four hours, they gave us a mess of *hogs' brains;* the hogs which they took on Groton banks when they plundered there. After being on board Thomas's sloop nearly three days, with nothing to eat or drink that we could swallow, we began to feel as if a struggle must be made, in some way, to prolong our existence, which after all our escapes, seemed still to be depending. In such a time, we can know for a reality how strong is the love of life. In the room where we were confined were a great many weapons of war, and some of the prisoners whispered that we might make a prize of the sloop. This in some way was overheard and got to the officer's ears, and now we were immediately put in a stronger place in the hold of the vessel; and they appeared so enraged that I was almost sure we should share a decisive fate, or suffer severely. Soon they commenced calling us, one by one, on deck. As I went up they seized me, tied my hands behind me with a strong rope-yarn, and drew it so tight that my shoulder-bones cracked and almost touched each other. Then a boat came from a fourteen-gun brig, commanded by one Steele. Into this boat I was ordered to get, without the use of my hands, over the sloop's bulwarks, which were all of three feet high, and

[5] The Tory part of Arnold's force was a detachment of two organizations—a party of the " American Legion " (commonly known as the Refugees) commanded by Lieut.-Col. Upham—one of the officers, Captain Samuel Wogan, was wounded,—and the Third Battalion of the New Jersey Volunteers, Alexander Van Buskirk, commanding.

then from these I had to fall, or throw myself into the boat. My distress of body and agitated feelings I cannot describe; and no relief could be anticipated, but only forebodings of a more severe fate. A prisoner with an enemy, an enraged and revengeful enemy, is a place where I pray my reader may never come. They made us all lie down under the seats on which the men sat to row, and so we were conveyed to the brig; going on board, we were ordered to stand in one rank by the gunwale, and in front of us was placed a spar, within about a foot of each man. Here we stood, with a sentry to each of us, having orders to shoot or bayonet us if we attempted to stir out of our place. All this time we had nothing to eat or drink, and it rained and was very cold. We were detained in this position about two hours, when we had liberty to go about the main deck. Night approached and we had no supper, nor anything to lie upon but the wet deck. We were on board this brig about four days, and then were removed on board a ship commanded by Captain Scott, who was very kind to the prisoners. He took me onto the quarter deck with him, and appeared to have the heart of a man. I should think he was about sixty years of age. I remained with him until I was exchanged. Captain Nathaniel Shaw came down to New York with the American flag, after me and four others who were prisoners with me, and belonged to Fort Griswold, and who were brave and fine young men. General Mifflin[6] went with the British flag to meet this American flag. I sailed with him about twenty miles. He asked me many questions, all of which I took caution how I answered, and gave him no information. I told him I was very sorry that he should come to destroy so many, many brave men, burn their property, distress so many families and make such desolation. I did not think they could be said to be honorable in so doing. He said, "We might thank our own countrymen for it." I told him I had no thanks for him. I then asked the General if

6 We have been unable to identify this British officer.—(Ed.)

I might ask him a few questions. "As many as you please." I asked him "how many of the army who made the attack upon New London and Groton were missing? As you, sir, are the commissary of the British army, I suppose you can tell." He replied, "that by the returns there were two hundred and twenty odd missing, but what had become of them he knew not." We advanced, and the flags met and I was exchanged and permitted to return home. Here I close my narrative; for, as I was requested, I have given a particular and unexaggerated account of that which I saw with mine own eyes.

RUFUS AVERY,

Orderly Sergeant under Captain William Latham.

RUFUS AVERY'S NARRATIVE

(From the original Ms.)

As I belonged to the garrison at Fort Griswold when Benedict Arnold's army came to New London and Groton on the sixth of September, 1781, and made their attack on both places, I had every opportunity to know all the movements through the day and time of the battle. I am requested to give a particular account of the conduct of the enemy. I had charge of the garrison the night before the enemy appeared anywhere near us, or were expected by anyone at that time to trouble us, but about three o'clock in the morning, as soon as I had daylight so as to see the fleet, it appeared a short distance below the lighthouse. The fleet consisted of thirty-two vessels in number—ships, brigs, schooners and sloops. I immediately sent word to Captain William Latham, who commanded the said fort and who was not far distant. He very soon came to the fort and saw the enemy's fleet, and immediately sent a notice to Colonel William Ledyard, who was commander of the harbor, Fort Griswold and Fort Trumbull. He soon arrived at the garrison, saw the fleet, then ordered two large guns to be loaded with heavy charges of good powder. Captain William Latham took charge of one gun that was discharged at the northeast part of the fort, and I took charge of the gun on the west side of the fort, so as to give a "larum" to the country in the best manner it could be done. We discharged then regular "larums." Two guns was the regular "larum," but the enemy understood that, and they discharged a third gun similar to ours and timed it alike, which broke our alarm, which discouraged our troops [from] coming to our assistance. Colonel William Ledyard immediately sent out two expresses, one from each fort, to call on every captain of a militia company of men, to hurry them to our relief; but not many came to our assistance. Their

568

excuse was that they supposed it to be only a false alarm. The discharge of the third gun by the enemy entirely changed the alarm. It was customary when a good prize was brought into the harbor, or on the receipt of any good news, to rejoice by discharging three cannon; and this the enemy understood. They landed eight hundred officers and men, and some horses and large guns and (gun) carriages on the beach at Eastern Point, Groton side of the river, about eight o'clock in the morning, and on New London side of the river below the lighthouse on the beach seven hundren officers and men at the same time. The army on the Groton side was divided into two divisions, about four hundred in each division. Colonel Eyre took command of the division southeast of the fort, about one hundred and thirty rods from the fort, behind a ledge of rocks. Major Montgomery took command of his division about one hundred and fifty rods from the fort, behind a high hill of land. The army on New London side of the river found better and more accommodating land for marching than on Groton side, and as soon as they got against Fort Trumbull they separated into two divisions. One went on to the town of New London, and plundered and set fire to the shipping and buildings, and the other division marched directly down to Fort Trumbull. Captain Shapley, who commanded the fort, saw that he was likely to be overpowered by the enemy, spiked up the cannon and embarked on board his boats, which were prepared for him and his men if wanted; but the enemy were so quick upon him that before he and his small company could get out of gunshot in their boats, a number of his men got badly wounded. Those who were able to get to Fort Griswold reached there, and most of them were slain. Colonel Eyre and Major Montgomery had their divisions stationed about nine o'clock in the morning. As soon as they appeared in sight we hove a number of shot at them, but they would endeavor to disappear immediately. About ten o'clock in the forenoon they sent their flag to demand of Colonel Ledyard the surrender of the fort. The party with the flag approached within about forty rods of the fort, and we discharged a musketball before them and brought them to a stand.   Colonel Ledyard called a council of war to take the minds of his fellow-officers and friends as to what was to be done.   They agreed to send a flag to meet theirs, and chose Captain Elijah Avery, Captain Amos Stanton and Captain John Williams.   They immediately met the British flag, and received a demand to give up the fort to them.   Our flag soon returned with the summons, which was to deliver the fort up to them.   Inquiry was made of the council as to what must be done, and the answer was sent to the British flag that the fort would not be given up. Their flag went back to Colonel Eyre's division and soon returned to within about seventy rods of the fort, when they were again met by our flag, which brought back to Colonel Ledyard the demand if they had to take the fort by storm they should put martial law in force; that is, whom they did not kill with balls should be put to death with sword and bayonet.   Our flag went to the British flag with Colonel Ledyard's answer that he should not give up the fort to them, let the consequence be what it might.   While the flags were passing between us we were exchanging shots with the British at Fort Trumbull, of which they had got possession before the commencement of the battle at Fort Griswold.   We could heave a shot into Fort Trumbull among the enemy without difficulty, but they could not raise so high as to come into Fort Griswold.   Having obtained possession of our good powder and shot left by Captain Shapley in the fort, they used it against us.   About eleven o'clock in the forenoon the enemy found out what we were determined to do.   Both divisions started; that of Colonel Eyre came on in solid column.   As soon as he got on level ground we were prepared to salute them with a gun that took in an eighteen pound ball, but was then loaded with two bags of grapeshot.   Captain Elias Henry Halsey directed the gun and took aim at the enemy. He had practiced on board of privateers, and he did his duty well. I was present with him and others near the gun, and when the shot struck among the enemy it cleared a wide space in their solid column. It was reported on good authority that about twenty men were killed and wounded by that charge of grapeshot. As soon as the enemy's column was broken by their loss of officers and men, they scattered, and trailed their arms and came on with a quick march and oblique step toward the fort, inclining to the west. During this time we hove cannon and musket shot among the enemy. Colonel Eyre's division came up to the south side and west side of the fort, where he was mortally wounded.[1] Major Montgomery, who started with his division at the same time that Eyre did to come to the fort in solid column, inclined to the north, until they got east of the redoubt or battery which is east of the fort, when a large number of them came very quick into the battery. Our officers threw a heavy charge of grapeshot among them, which destroyed a large number. They then started for the fort, a part of them in platoons, discharging their guns as they advanced, while some scattering officers and soldiers came round to the east and north part of the fort. As soon as the enemy got round the fort one man attempted to open the gate. He lost his life. There was hard fighting some time before the second man made the trial to open the gate, which he did. Our little number of one hundred and fifty-five officers and soldiers, most of whom were volunteers when the battle began, were soon overpowered. Then there was no blockhouse on the parade as there is now, and the enemy had every opportunity to kill and wound almost every man in the fort. When they had overpowered us and driven us from our stations at the breastwork of the fort, Colonel William Ledyard seeing what few officers and men he had left to do any more fighting, they quit their posts and went on the open parade in the fort, where the enemy had every opportunity to massacre us, as there was about six of the enemy to one of us. The enemy mounted the parapet seemingly all as one, swung their hats around once, and discharged their guns, and them they did not kill with ball they meant to kill with the bayonet. I was on the west side of the fort with Captain Ed-

[1] A mistake—he survived, to die many years later.

ward Latham and Mr. Christopher Latham on the platform; had a full sight of the enemy's conduct and within five feet of these two men. I had at that time a ball and bayonet hole in my coat. As soon as the enemy discharged their guns they knocked down the two men before-mentioned with the breech of their guns, and put their bayonets into them, but did not quite kill them. By this time Major Montgomery's division, then under the command of Captain Bromfield (the other gates having been unbolted by one of the men) marched in through the gates and formed a solid column. At this time I left my station on the west side of the fort and went across the south part of the parade towards the south end of the barrack. Colonel William Ledyard was on the parade, marching towards the enemy under Captain Bromfield, raising and lowering his sword. He was then about six or eight feet from British officer. I turned my eyes from Ledyard and stepped up to the door of the barrack, and saw the enemy discharging their guns through the windows. I turned myself immediately about, and the enemy had executed Colonel Ledyard in less time than one minute after I saw him. The column then continued marching toward the south end of the parade. I could do no better than to pass across the parade before the enemy's column, as they discharged the volleys of three platoons, the fire of which I went through. I believe there was not less than five or six hundred men of the enemy on the parade in the fort. They killed and wounded nearly every man in the fort as quick as they could, which was done in about one minute. I expected my time to come with the rest. One mad-looking fellow put his bayonet to my side and swore "by—— he would skipper me." I looked him very earnestly in the face and eyes, and asked for mercy and to spare my life. He attempted three times to put the bayonet in me, but I must say I believe God forbade him, for I was completely in his power, as well as others that was present with the enemy. The enemy at the same time massacred Lieutenant Enoch Stanton within four or five feet of me. A platoon of about ten men marched up near where I stood, where two large outer doors to the magazine made a space wide enough for ten men to stand in one rank. They discharged their guns into the magazine among the dead and wounded and some well ones, and some they killed and wounded. That platoon fell back and another platoon came forward to discharge their guns into the outer part of the magazine where the others did. As they made ready to fire Captain Bromfield came suddenly round the corner of the magazine, and very quickly raised his sword, exclaiming "stop firing! You'll send us all to hell together." (Their language was bad as well as their conduct; I was near him when he spoke.) Bromfield knew, there must be, of course, much powder scattered about the magazine and a great quantity deposited there; but I expect the reason it did not take fire was that there was so much human blood to put it out. They did not bayonet many after they ceased firing their guns. I was amongst them all the time, and they very soon left off killing, and then went stripping and robbing the dead and wounded, and also those that were not wounded. They then ordered each one of us to march out to the northeast part of the parade, and them that could not go themselves from their wounds, were to be helped by those that were well. Mr. Samuel Edgcomb, Jr., and myself were ordered to take Ensign Charles Eldredge out of the magazine. He was a very large, heavy man, who had been shot in the knee joint. We poor prisoners were taken out on the parade about two rods from the gate of the fort, and every man ordered to sit down immediately—and if not obeyed at once the bayonet was to be put into him. The battle was then finished, which was about one o'clock in the afternoon; the enemy began to take care of their dead and wounded. The first thing they did was to take off six of the outer doors of the barrack, and with four men to a door would bring in one man at a time on each door. There were twenty-four men at work about two hours, as fast as they could walk and deposit them on the west side of the parade in the fort, where it was the most comfortable place they could find, while we poor prisoners were put in the most uncomfortable spot on the parade in the fort, where the sun shone down so very warm on us that it made us feel more unhappy. Some of the wounded men lay dying. Captain Youngs Ledyard and Captain Nathan Moore were among the number. I sat on the ground with the other prisoners and these two fine men lay on the ground by me, Ledyard's head on one thigh and Moore's head on the other. They both died that night. While I was with them they had their reason, and requested water for their thirst. I asked of the enemy water for my brother prisoners to drink, as well as for myself. They granted my request. The well was within two rods of us. I watched them when they brought the water to me for us to drink, to see that they did not put anything in it to poison us; for they had repeatedly said that we must all die before the sun went down, because that was in the summons sent to Colonel William Ledyard, that those who were not killed by the musket ball should die by the sword and bayonet. But happy for us that was alive they did not offer to hurt any one man, and they said that was a falsehood. They kept us on the ground in the garrison about two hours after the battle was over, and then ordered every man that was able to walk, rise up immediately. Sentries with loaded guns and fixed bayonets were placed around us, with orders to shoot or bayonet anyone that did not obey the officer. I was obliged to leave two dying men that were resting on me as they lay on the ground beside me. We marched down on the bank by the river so as to be ready to embark to go on board the British fleet. Then, about thirty of us, every man was ordered to sit down, and as at other times was surrounded by sentries. Captain Bromfield came and took the names of the wounded who were able to march down with us. I sat where I had a fair view of the enemy's conduct. The sun was about half an hour high, and they were setting fire to the buildings and bringing down plunder by us as we were placed at the lower part of the village. At the same time a large number of the enemy between us and the fort were getting ready to quit the ground. They loaded up our very large, heavy ammunition wagon that belonged to the fort with the wounded men who could not go themselves, and about twenty of the soldiers drew it out of the fort and brought it to the brow of the hill on which the fort stood, which was very steep and about thirty rods distance. As soon as the enemy began to move the wagon down the hill, they began to put themselves in a position to hold it back with all their power. They found it too much for them to do; they released their hold on the wagon as quick as possible to prevent being run over by the wagon themselves, leaving it to run down the hill with great speed. It ran about twelve rods to a large apple-tree stump, and both shafts of the wagon struck very hard and hurt the wounded men very much. A great number of the enemy were near where the wagons stopped, and they immediately ran to the wagon and brought that and the wounded men by where we prisoners were sitting on the ground, and deposited them in the house nearby, that belonged to Ensign Ebenezer Avery, who was one that was in the wagon when it started down the hill. Some of the enemy had set fire to the house before the wounded prisoners were placed in it, but the fire was put out by some of the others. Captain Bromfield paroled the wounded men who were left, and took Ebenezer Ledward, Esq., as a hostage for them left on parole, to see them forthcoming if called for. By this time the enemy's boats came up to the shore near where we prisoners were. The officers spoke with a doleful sound: "Come you rebels, go on board the boats." That touched my feelings more than anything that passed for the day. I realized that I should have to leave my dear wife and my good neighbors and friends, and also my native land, and suffer with cold and hunger, as I was in the power of a cruel foe or enemy; but I was still in the hands of a higher Power, which was a great consolation to me, for I am sensible that God has preserved my life through many hardships, and when in danger of losing my life many times in the wars, etc. When we prisoners had marched down to the shore, the boats that were to receive us were kept off where the water was about knee deep, and we were marched down in two ranks, one on each side of the boat. The officer that had the command very harshly ordered us to "get on board immediately." There were about twelve prisoners in a boat. They rowed us down to an armed sloop commanded by one Captain Thomas as they called him, a refugee Tory, who lay with his vessel within the fleet. As soon as they put us on board the sloop they sent us down in the hold of the vessel, where they had a fire for cooking which made it very hot and smoky. They stopped up the hatchway, making it so close that we had no air to breathe. We begged that they would spare our lives, and they gave us some relief by opening the hatchway and letting one or two of us come on deck at a time during the night, but with sentries with guns and bayonets to watch us. They did not give us anything to eat or drink for about twenty-four hours, and then only a mess made of hog's brains that they caught on Groton bank, with other plunder. While we were on board Thomas' sloop we had nothing to eat or drink that we could hardly swallow. This continued about three days. There were a number of weapons of war where we were placed in the vessel, and some of the prisoners whispered together that there was an opportunity to make a prize of the sloop. This somehow got to the officers' ears, and they immediately shut us all down in the hold of the vessel. I felt very certain that we would have to suffer, for they seemed so enraged that they appeared to have an intention to massacre us all. They soon got ready, and began to call us upon deck one by one. As I came up they tied my hands behind me with strong rope yarns, binding them together; and winding the rope yarn so hard as to nearly bring my shoulder blades to touch each other. Then they had a boat come from a fourteen-gun brig commanded by a Captain Steel, by name and nature. I was ordered to get over the side of the sloop without the use of my hands, the bulwarks above the deck being all of three feet in height, and then I had to fall into the boat that was to carry us to the brig and was made to lay down under the seats on which the rowers sat, as though we were brutes about to be slaughtered. After we were put on board the brig we were ordered to stand in one rank beside the gunwale of the vessel, and a spar was placed before us leaving about one foot space for each man to stand in, with a sentry to nearly every man, with orders to bayonet or shoot anyone that offered to move. They kept us in that situation about two hours in the rain and cold, with very thin clothing upon us, and then gave us liberty to go about the main deck, and were obliged to lie on the wet deck without anything to eat or drink for supper. We were on board the brig about four days, and then put on board a ship commanded by Captain Scott, who appeared very friendly to we prisoners. He took me on the quarter deck with him. He was apparently about sixty years of age, and I remained with him until I was exchanged. Captain Nathaniel Shaw came down to New York with the American flag [of truce] after me and four young men that were made prisoners with me that belonged to the garrison at Fort Griswold, and during the time of the battle behaved like good soldiers. General Mifflin[1] came with the British flag to meet the American flag. I sailed with him about twenty miles in the flag-boat.[2] He asked me some questions, but I gave him little or no information, and told him I was very sorry that they came to destroy so many good men and cause so much distress to families and desolation in the community, by burning so much valuable property; and further, that I did not believe they would gain any honor by it. He replied we might thank our own countrymen for it. I told him I should not. I then turned to the General and said: "Will you answer me a few questions?" "As many as you please, Sir," was his reply. I made many inquiries, and asked

[1] No such name appears in the British army lists.

[2] The mention by Avery of "sailing twenty miles in the flag-boat" probably refers to the incident noted in the *Connecticut Gazette* of September 21, 1781:
"Monday . . . a flag sailed from hence with five of Arnold's burning party that were taken prisoners here; the flag overtook the fleet at Whitestone, and returned here last Sunday with five lads that were taken at Fort Griswold."

him how many of the enemy was missing that were engaged in the attack on Groton and New London, remarking: " Sir, I expect you can tell, as you are the Commissary of the British army." He said, "I find in the returns that there were two hundred and twenty odd missing, but I don't know what became of them." Here I conclude the foregoing particular account from my own personal knowledge of the British attack and capture of Fort Griswold, and their brutal conduct at New London and Groton, and also of their barbarous treatment of the prisoners who fell into their hands.

RUFUS AVERY,

Orderly-Sergeant, under Captain William Latham, who commanded the Matross Company at Fort Griswold, Sept. 6, 1781.

KILLED AND MORTALLY WOUNDED OF GROTON

Lieut.-Col. William Ledyard
Christopher Avery
Elijah Avery
Ebenezer Avery
Daniel Avery
David Avery
Elisha Avery
Jasper Avery
Solomon Avery
Thomas Avery
Nathaniel Adams
Benadam Allen
Belton Allen
Samuel Allen
Simeon Allen
Ezekiel Bailey
Andrew Baker
John P. Babcock
Andrew Billings

John Brown
Hubbart Burrows
Daniel Chester
Jeremiah Chester
Philip Covil
Samuel Hill
Rufus Hurlbut
Moses Jones
Barney Kinne
John Lester
Jonas Lester
Wait Lester
Joseph Lewis
Wait Ledyard
Youngs Ledyard
Edward Mills
Thomas Miner
Simeon Morgan
Nathan Moor

Joseph Moxley
David Palmer
Asa Perkins
Elisha Perkins
Elnathan Perkins
Luke Perkins
Luke Perkins, Jr.
Simeon Perkins
David Seabury
Nathan Sholes
Amos Stanton

Nicholas Starr
Thomas Starr, Jr.
John Stedman
Solomon Tift
Sylvester Walworth
Patrick Ward
Josiah Wigger
Henry Williams
Christopher Woodbridge
Henry Woodbridge

OF NEW LONDON

Samuel Billings
William Bolton
Jonathan Butler
Richard Chapman
John Clark
James Comstock (75 years old)
William Comstock

John Holt
Eliaday Jones
Peter Richards
Daniel Williams (15 years old)
John Whittelsey
Stephen Whittelsey

OF STONINGTON

Daniel Stanton
Thomas Williams

Enoch Stanton

OF PRESTON

John Billings

OF LONG ISLAND

—— Ellis   Henry Halsey
(Probably the same man—Elias Henry Halsey.)

NEGROES

Jordan Freeman   Lambo Latham (not "Sambo")
61 British were buried at Groton.

579

NARRATIVE OF STEPHEN HEMPSTEAD

T HE author of the following narrative of events entered the service of his country in 1775, and arrived in Boston on the day of the battle of Bunker Hill. He was at Dorchester Point, was on Long Island at the time of the retreat of the American army and was also a volunteer in the fire ships that were sent to destroy the *Asia,* eighty-four-gun ship, and a frigate lying above Fort Washington. In this attempt they were unsuccessful, although grappled to the enemy's vessel twenty minutes. For the bravery displayed by them they received the particular thanks of the commanding officer, in person and in general orders, and forty dollars were ordered to be paid to each person engaged. He was afterwards wounded by a grapeshot while defending the lines at Harlem Heights, which broke two of his ribs. He continued in the service, and was again wounded on the 6th of September, 1781. He is now more than seventy-six years of age. He formerly resided in New London. He enjoyed the reception of General Lafayette in that place during his last visit to this country, and has within a few years written this account in full, for publication:

On the morning of the 6th of September, 1781, twenty-four sail of the enemy's shipping appeared to the westward of New London harbor. The enemy landed in two divisions, of about eight hundred men each, commanded by that infamous traitor to his country, Benedict Arnold, who headed the division that landed on the New London side, near Brown's farms; the other division, commanded by Colonel Ayres,[1] landed on Groton Point, nearly opposite. I was first sergeant of Captain Adam Shapley's company of State troops, and was stationed with him at the time, with about twenty-three men, at Fort Trumbull, on the New London

[1] Eyre.

580

side. This was a mere breastwork or water battery, open from behind, and the enemy coming on us from that quarter we spiked our cannon, and commenced a retreat across the river to Fort Griswold in three boats. The enemy was so near that they overshot us with their muskets, and succeeded in capturing one boat with six men commanded by Josiah Smith, a private. They afterwards proceeded to New London and burnt the town. We were received by the garrison with enthusiasm, being considered experienced artillerists whom they much needed; and we were immediately assigned to our stations. The fort was an oblong square, with bastions at opposite angles, its longest side fronting the river in a N. W. and S. E. direction. Its walls were of stone, and were ten or twelve feet high on the lower side and surrounded by a ditch. On the wall were pickets, projecting over twelve feet; above this was a parapet with embrasures, and within a platform for the cannon, and a step to mount upon, to shoot over the parapet with small arms. In the S. W. bastion was a flagstaff, and in the side near the opposite angle was the gate, in front of which was a triangular breastwork to protect the gate; and to the right of this was a redoubt, with a three-pounder in it, which was about one hundred and twenty yards from the gate. Between the fort and the river was another battery, with a covered way, but which could not be used in this attack, as the enemy appeared in a different quarter. The garrison, with the volunteers, consisted of about one hundred and sixty men. Soon after our arrival the enemy appeared in force in some woods about half a mile S. E. of the fort, from whence they sent a flag of truce, which was met by Captain Shapley, demanding an unconditional surrender, threatening at the same time, to storm the fort instantly, if the terms were not accepted. A council of war was held, and it was the unanimous voice that the garrison were unable to defend themselves against so superior a force. But a militia Colonel who was then in the fort and had a body of men in the immediate vicinity, said he would reinforce them with two or three hundred men in fifteen minutes, if they would hold out; Colonel Ledyard agreed to send back a defiance, upon the most solemn assurance of immediate succour. For this purpose, Colonel —— started, his men being then in sight; but he was no more seen, nor did he even attempt a diversion in our favor. When the answer to their demand had been returned by Captain Shapley, the enemy were soon in motion and marched with great rapidity, in a solid column, to within a short distance of the fort, where dividing the column, they rushed furiously and simultaneously to the assault of the S. W. bastion and the opposite sides. They were, however, repulsed with great slaughter, their commander mortally wounded, and Major Montgomery, next in rank, killed, having been thrust through the body whilst in the act of scaling the walls at the S. W. bastion, by Captain Shapley. The command then devolved on Colonel Beckwith,[1] a refugee from New Jersey, who commanded a corps of that description. The enemy rallied and returned the attack with great vigor, but were received and repulsed with equal firmness. During the attack a shot cut the halyards of the flag and it fell to the ground, but was instantly remounted on a pike pole. This accident proved fatal to us, as the enemy supposed it had been struck by its defenders, rallied again, and rushing with redoubled impetuosity carried the S. W. bastion by storm. Until this moment, our loss was trifling in number, being six or seven killed and eighteen or twenty wounded. Never was a post more bravely defended, nor a garrison more barbarously butchered. We fought with all kinds of weapons and at all places, with a courage that deserved a better fate. Many of the enemy were killed under the walls by throwing simple shot over on them, and never would we have relinquished our arms had we had the least idea that such a catastrophe would have followed. To describe this scene I must be permitted to go back a little in my narrative. I commanded an eighteen-pounder on the south side of the gate, and while in the act of sighting my gun a ball

[1] A mistake. Beckwith was a British officer. He may have meant Van Buskirk.

passed through the embrasure, struck me a little above the right ear, grazing the skull and cutting off the veins, which bled profusely. A handkerchief was tied around it and I continued at my duty. Discovering some little time after, that a British soldier had broken a picket at the bastion on my left, and was forcing himself through the hole, whilst the men stationed there were gazing at the battle which raged opposite to them, I cried, "My brave fellows, the enemy are breaking in behind you," and raised my pike to despatch the intruder, when a ball struck my left arm at the elbow and my pike fell to the ground. Nevertheless I grasped it with my right hand, and with the men, who turned and fought manfully, cleared the breach. The enemy, however, soon after forced the S. W. bastion, where Captain Shapley, Captain Peter Richards, Lieutenant Richard Chapman and several other men of distinction, and volunteers, had fought with unconquerable courage, and were all either killed or mortally wounded, and which had sustained the brunt of every attack.

Captain P. Richards, Lieutenant Chapman and several others were killed in the bastion; Captain Shapley and others wounded. He died of his wounds in January following.

Colonel Ledyard, seeing the enemy within the fort, gave orders to cease firing, and to throw down our arms, as the fort had surrendered. We did so, but they continued firing upon us, crossed the fort and opened the gate, when they marched in, firing in platoons upon those who were retreating to the magazine and barrack rooms for safety. At this moment the renegade Colonel Bromfield[1] commanding, cried out, "Who commands this garrison?" Colonel Ledyard, who was standing near me, answered, "I did, sir, but you do now," at the same time stepping forward, handed him his sword with the point towards himself. At this instant I perceived a soldier in the act of bayoneting me from behind. I turned suddenly round and grasped his bayonet, endeav-

[1] Bloomfield or Bromfield.

oring to unship it, and knock off the thrust—but in vain. I having but one hand, he succeeded in forcing it into my right hip, above the joint and just below the abdomen, and crushed me to the ground. The first person I saw afterwards was my brave commander a corpse by my side, having been run through the body with his own sword by the savage renegade. Never was a scene of more brutal, wanton carnage witnessed, than now took place. The enemy were still firing upon us in platoons and in the barrack rooms, which were continued for some minutes, when they discovered they were in danger of being blown up, by communicating fire to the powder scattered at the mouth of the magazine, while delivering out cartridges; nor did it then cease in the rooms for some minutes longer. All this time the bayonet was "freely used," even on those who were helplessly wounded and in the agonies of death. I recollect Captain William Seymour, a volunteer from Hartford, had thirteen bayonet wounds, although his knee had previously been shattered by a ball, so much so that it was obliged to be amputated the next day. But I need not mention particular cases. I have already said that we had six killed and eighteen wounded previous to their storming our lines; eighty-five were killed in all, thirty-five mortally and dangerously wounded, and forty taken prisoners to New York, most of them slightly hurt.

After the massacre they plundered us of everything we had, and left us literally naked. When they commenced gathering us up together with their own wounded, they put theirs under the shade of the platform and exposed us to the sun in front of the barracks, where we remained over an hour. Those that could stand were then paraded and ordered to the landing, while those that could not (of which number I was one), were put in one of our ammunition wagons, and taken to the brow of the hill (which was very steep, and at least one hundred rods in descent,) from whence it was permitted[1] to run down by itself, but was arrested in

[1] This does not agree with Avery's story.

its course, near the river, by an apple tree. The pain and anguish we all endured in this rapid descent as the wagon jumped and jostled over rocks and holes is inconceivable; and the jar in its arrest was like bursting the cords of life asunder, and caused us to shriek with almost supernatural force. Our cries were distinctly heard and noticed on the opposite side of the river (which is a mile wide), amidst all the confusion which raged in burning and sacking the town. We remained in the wagon more than an hour, before our humane conquerors hunted us up, when we were again paraded and laid on the beach, preparatory to embarkation. But by the interposition of Ebenezer Ledyard (brother to Colonel L.), who humanely represented our deplorable situation, and the impossibility of our being able to reach New York, thirty-five of us were paroled in the usual form. Being near the house of Ebenezer Avery, who was also one of our number, we were taken into it. Here we had not long remained before a marauding party set fire to every room, evidently intending to burn us up with the house. The party soon left it, when it was with difficulty extinguished and we were thus saved from the flames. Ebenezer Ledyard again interfered and obtained a sentinel to remain and guard us until the last of the enemy embarked, about eleven o'clock at night. None of our own people came to us till near daylight the next morning, not knowing previous to that time that the enemy had departed.

Such a night of distress and anguish was scarcely ever passed by mortal. Thirty-five of us were lying on the bare floor—stiff, mangled and wounded in every manner, exhausted with pain, fatigue and loss of blood, without clothes or anything to cover us, trembling with cold and spasms of extreme anguish, without fire or light, parched with excruciating thirst, not a wound dressed nor a soul to administer to one of our wants, nor an assisting hand to turn us during these long tedious hours of the night; nothing but groans and unavailing sighs were heard, and two of our number did not live to see the light of morning, which brought with it some ministering angels to our relief. The first was in the person of Miss Fanny Ledyard, of Southold, L. I., then on a visit to her uncle, our murdered commander, who held to my lips a cup of warm chocolate, and soon after returned with wine and other refreshments, which revived us a little. For these kindnesses she has never ceased to receive my most grateful thanks and fervent prayers for her felicity.

The cruelty of our enemy cannot be conceived, and our renegade countrymen surpassed in this respect, if possible, our British foes. We were at least an hour after the battle, within a few steps of a pump in the garrison, well supplied with water, and, although we were suffering with thirst they would not permit us to take one drop of it, nor give us any themselves. Some of our number, who were not disabled from going to the pump, were repulsed with the bayonet, and not one drop did I taste after the action commenced, although begging for it after I was wounded of all who came near me, until relieved by Miss Ledyard. We were a horrible sight at this time. Our own friends did not know us— even my own wife came in the room in search of me and did not recognize me, and as I did not see her, she left the room to seek for me among the slain, who had been collected under a large elm tree near the house. It was with the utmost difficulty that many of them could be identified, and we were frequently called upon to assist their friends in distinguishing them, by remembering particular wounds, &c. Being myself taken out by two men for this purpose I met my wife and brother, who after my wounds were dressed by Dr. Downer, from Preston, took me—not to my own home, for that was in ashes, as also every article of my property, furniture and clothing—but to my brother's,[1] where I lay eleven months as helpless as a child, and to this day feel the effects of it severely.

[1] The Hempstead house was one of the very few spared by the British, it is said because finding dinner on the table, they sat down to eat.

Such was the battle of Groton Heights; and such, as far as my imperfect manner and language can describe, a part of the sufferings which we endured. Never for a moment have I regretted the share I had in it; I would for an equal degree of honour, and the prosperity which has resulted to my country from the Revolution, be willing, if possible, to suffer it again.

STEPHEN HEMPSTEAD.

NAMES OF THE HEROES WHO FELL AT FORT GRISWOLD

SEPTEMBER 6TH, 1781.

Colonel William Ledyard, Groton.
David Avery, Esq.,   do.
Captain John Williams,   do.
Captain Simeon Allyn,   do.
Captain Samuel Allyn,   do.
Captain Elisha Avery,   do.
Captain Amos Stanton,   do.
Captain Elijah Avery,   do.
Captain Hubbard Burrows,   do.
Captain Youngs Ledyard,   do.
Captain Nathan More,   do.
Captain Joseph Lewis,   do.
Lieutenant Ebenezer Avery,   do.
Lieutenant Henry Williams,   do.
Lieutenant Patrick Ward,   do.
Lieutenant John Lester,   do.
Ensign Daniel Avery,   do.
Sergeant John Stedman,   do.
Sergeant Solomon Avery,   do.
Sergeant Jasper Avery,   do.
Sergeant Ezekiel Bailey,   do.
Sergeant Rufus Hurlburt,   do.
Sergeant Christopher Avery,   do.

Sergeant Eldridge Chester, Groton.
Sergeant Nicholas Starr,   do.
Corporal Edward Mills,   do.
Corporal Luke Perkins, Jr.,   do.
Corporal Andrew Billings,   do.
Corporal Simeon Morgan,   do.
Corporal Nathan Sholes,   do.
Daniel Chester,   do.
Thomas Avery,   do.
David Palmer,   do.
Sylvester Walworth,   do.
Philip Covel,   do.
Jedediah Chester,   do.
David Seabury,   do.
Henry Woodbridge,   do.
Christopher Woodbridge,   do.
Elnathan Perkins,   do.
Luke Perkins,   do.
Elisha Perkins,   do.
John Brown,   do.
John P. Babcock,   do.
Nathaniel Adams,   do.
Waite Lester,   do.
Samuel Hill,   do.
Joseph Moxley,   do.
Thomas Starr, Jr.,   do.
Moses Jones,   do.
Belton Allyn,   do.
Benjamin Allyn,   do.
Jonas Lester,   do.
Thomas Miner,   do.
Andrew Baker,   do.
Joseph Wiger,   do.
Samuel Billings,   do.

Eli Jones,   Groton.
Thomas Lamb,   do.
Frederick Chester,   do.
Daniel Davis,   do.
Daniel D. Lester,   do.
Captain Adam Shapley, New London.
Captain Peter Richards,   do.
Benoni Kenson,   do.
James Comstock,   do.
Richard Chapman,   do.
John Holt,   do.
John Clarke,   do.
Jonathan Butler,   do.
John Whittelsey,   do.
Stephen Whittelsey,   do.
William Bolton,   do.
William Comstock,   do.
Elias Coit,   do.
Barney Kinney,   do.
Captain Elias Henry Halsey, Long Island.
Lieutenant Enoch Stanton, Stonington.
Sergeant Daniel Stanton,   do.
Thomas Williams,   do.
Lamb Latham, (Colored).
Jordan Freeman,   do.

NAMES OF THE WOUNDED, PAROLED AND LEFT AT HOME

BY CAPTAIN BLOOMFIELD.

Captain William Latham, wounded in the thigh, Groton.
Captain Solomon Perkins, in the face,   do.
Captain Edward Latham, in the body,   do.
Lieutenant P. Avery, lost an eye,   do.
Lieutenant Obadiah Perkins, in the breast,   do.

Lieutenant William Starr, in the breast,	Groton.
Ensign Charles Eldridge, in the knee,	do.
Ensign Joseph Woodmaney, lost an eye,	do.
Ensign Ebenezer Avery, in the head,	do.
John Morgan, shot through the knee,	do.
Sanford Williams, shot in the body,	do.
John Daboll, shot in the head,	do.
Samuel Edgecomb, Jr., in the hand,	do.
Jabish Pendleton, in the hand,	do.
Asahel Woodworth, in the neck,	do.
Thomas Woodworth, in the leg,	do.
Ebenezer Perkins, in the face,	do.
Daniel Eldridge, in the neck and face,	do.
Christopher Latham, in the body,	do.
Christopher Eldridge, in the face,	do.
Amos Avery, in the hand,	do.
T. Woodworth, in the knee,	do.
Frederick Wave,[1] in the body,	do.
Elisha Prior, in the arm,	do.
Sergeant Daniel Stanton, in the body,	Stonington.
Corporal — Judd, shot in the knee,	Hebron.
William Seymour, lost his leg,	Hartford.

[1] This should undoubtedly be *Moore*.

APPENDIX

BENEDICT ARNOLD, it is well known, was a native of Connecticut, and, by his knowledge of the situation of this seaport and fortress was capable of conducting the British up to its shores, which, it is probable they would not have hazarded had they not had a good pilot.

It may be instructing to those in a distant part of the country, into whose hands these pages may fall, to observe, that New London is one of the best seaports in Connecticut, with a most excellent harbor, being but about three miles up the mouth of the Thames, which falls into Long Island Sound, which has a broad communication with the ocean. The Thames is a water communication between New London and Norwich fourteen miles north. It flows in a valley between the two elevated portions of land, New London on its west side, and Groton on its east. The land on the east of this stream rises to a sublime elevation, commanding a fair view of nearly the whole sound; on this hill stood the Fort Griswold of which our narrative describes the capture; and on its site is now erected a splendid monument, inscribed with the names of the brave heroes, who gave their lives to save their country.

The following particulars of Arnold's escape from the demands of justice, and the manner in which he effected his desertion, were obtained from an eye witness, and serve still further to explain the whole transaction.

Mr. Ebenezer Chase was a private in the New Hampshire militia, which relieved the line of Pennsylvania, at West Point in 1780, when those troops were veteran and were needed elsewhere. Mr. Chase, with several others, being off duty, was on the shore of the Hudson when Arnold deserted.   When General Washington assigned the command of West Point to Arnold, he left the barge in his possession.   A temporary hut was erected on the east shore, for accommodation of the four oarsmen who managed the barge.   On the morning of his desertion, Arnold rode down from his headquarters, to the shore, very fast, threw the reins to his attendant, and ordered the barge to be manned.   He directed his course towards the Point; but, on reaching the middle of the river, the boat was observed to take a different direction and move down the stream with great rapidity.   The explanation was afterwards thus made by the barge men.   "He hoisted a flag of truce, and told them to pull for the *Vulture* (British sloop of war), saying he had business with the captain.   He promised them if they would row him down to the *Vulture* with speed, he would give each of them a guinea and a gallon of rum.   On nearing the sloop, and being within range of her guns, he opened his plan to them, saying, "I have served the ungrateful scoundrels long enough;" and declaring if they would go with him, they should have double pay, and they should be made officers in the British service."   One of them replied that "he did not understand fighting on both sides."

"Then," said Arnold, "you are prisoners!"   Arnold ascended the deck and was received by the marines with presented arms: he then ordered his men to come on board, as prisoners of war. One of them said, "It was a shabby trick, as they had toiled so hard to get along, now to refuse the promised reward, and make them prisoners."   The English Captain heard this, and stepping forward, observed, "General Arnold, I command this vessel, and while I walk this quarterdeck, no such mean transaction shall take place here."   Then addressing the boatmen continued, "My good fellows, I respect your principles of honor, and fidelity to your country, although you are enemies to your King; you shall have the liberty to go or stay as you choose."   Here (taking from his purse the money), "are your promised guineas;—steward, put up four gallons of rum for these men." The boatmen thanked the gallant sailor, for his generosity and justice, and returned in safety to headquarters, and reported the proceedings to General Washington, who had just returned to camp. Arnold, during the conversation on board, retired to the cabin enraged and chagrined.

This statement was made by Chase about a fortnight before his death, in 1831. He also stated that he saw the unfortunate André going to execution. The cause of Arnold's desertion was that the poor deluded Major André was taken; information being sent him by the person himself. Arnold manifested an inveterate hatred of his country, as his succeeding conduct evidently exhibited, till the close of hostilities. After the war, he went to England, where he was despised, and died chagrined and wretched. It is related, that the unfeeling wretch called on the widowed mother and sister of his unfortunate victim (André) announcing his name to the servant: but they returned answer that "they had no desire to see him."

ANECDOTE OF MRS. BAILEY

IT will be interesting to the reader to hear that there still lives, on Groton banks, the zealous old lady who gave her *flannel petticoat,* in the emergency of the capture of the fort. She is a real heroine of the "old school," and at this advanced age, re- hearses that event with all the enthusiasm of youth. She is much interested in all the subjects which agitate the political world, and possesses considerable correct information. She is visited by the great, and indulges their curiosity by telling the oft-repeated tale, which she does with a pathos, that excites admiration. And so novel is the fact, though recorded on historic page, that many re- quest her to relate it that they may have to say, "I have seen Mrs. Bailey [1] who gave the petticoat." She says, "In the heat of ac- tion there came a soldier, rushing into my apartment, saying 'for God's sake give us some flannel for cartridges!' " "I will," said I. "Here is a blanket, 'tis all I have,"—but that moment recol- lecting her garment, she hastily unpinned the same, and handed it to the man, "who flew to his post," &c. Thus she has immortal- ized her name, as a zealous lover of her country.

[1] The local Chapter of the Daughters of the American Revolution, which has Fort Gris- wold in its care is named the ANNA WARNER BAILEY Chapter.

For a portrait of Mrs. Bailey, who died in 1851 at the age of 92, see Lossing's *Field- Book of the Revolution.*—(ED.)

EULOGY ON GENERAL WASHINGTON

WASHINGTON, whose immortal name stands recorded on the historic page, first and greatest of men, and who led the American forces through the eight years' most trying struggle, now lies mouldering with the dust of Mount Vernon; and his choice spirit is with God. We think there could never be combined in one man, so many excellent and superior qualities as signalized our venerated Commander-in-Chief,— a great hero,—a most wise and judicious counsellor in war and in peace,—a pleasant friend and neighbor in his domestic retreat,— a Christian,—possessed of the finest feelings of humanity and mercy. Washington was a man of prayer. Often, during the war, and particularly when preparing for an attack, he was seen by his Aids and attendants to retire and pray; imploring the assistance and direction of the God of Justice, and His omnipotent arm of defence against oppression.

His peculiar humanity and sympathy, appeared in the case of the unfortunate André. He deeply regretted the necessity of putting to death that fine officer in the flower of his days; and, too, when he was not the malicious instigator, but only the agent for another's crime. It is related that Washington often sent him a meal from his own table while he lay in prison; and at his melancholy execution, where thousands flocked for curiosity and to gaze unfeelingly on that appalling spectacle of human woe, the benevolent, the noble-hearted Washington, and his guards would not appear. General Washington's name and virtues ought to be enshrined in the hearts of his countrymen, as the rolling ocean of time will soon eradicate from Mount Vernon and from earth, the last of his family; for he had no descendants. He married a Mrs. Custis, a widow, and bequeathed the most of his estate to his nephew, Colonel Bushrod Washington.

But we are led to believe that all the virtues which constituted a George Washington, died not with him. No, our country has now on the stage of political action, the veteran heart, the judicious mind and ardent lover of freedom and independence. And in case of an invasion of a foreign foe, it would be found that the sons inherited the blood of their fathers, and that Bunker Hill, and Groton, and New London's ashes were not forgotten.

> Hail to the land whereon we tread,
>   Our fondest boast;
> The sepulchre of mighty dead,
> The truest hearts that ever bled,
> Who sleep on glory's bed,
>   A fearless host.
>
> Let foreign navies hasten o'er,
> And on our heads their fury pour,
> And peal their cannon's loudest roar,
>   And storm our land;
> They still shall find our lives are given,
>   To die for Home!

Advance, now, ye future generations! We would hail you, as you rise in your long succession to fill the places which we now fill, and to taste the blessings of freedom and independence, which we now are passing through. We bid you welcome to this pleasant, but dear-bought land of your fathers. We bid you welcome to the healthful skies and verdant fields of New England. Welcome to the benevolent and very hospitable hearts and homes, of the pleasant villages of New London and Groton. View, and read on the recently erected monuments the names of those who bled for your safety; and let the recollection of the scenes sketched in the preceding pages, aid your sympathetic reflections. The soil is respread with the pleasant verdure of many peaceful years; —the gore is absorbed in the earth, and the placid and beautiful Thames, which was disturbed with the rushing of a host of enemies and stained with the life-drops of the slain, now rolls onward in peace, to its home in the ocean. So have passed away the preceding generations, till 1841 finds but few remaining who can say, they saw the battle of '76, or of '81.

Let us cherish sentiments of humanity and universal philanthropy, and detest *war,* for the sake of extending power or of enlarging our territories beyond the limits of justice and right;—but prove our attachment to the cause of good government, and civil and religious liberty, by unwearied efforts in defence of our country and a strict adherence to our invaluable Constitution: remembering the motto of our esteemed Washington, "United we stand,—divided we fall."

War and peace contrasted, must fix on the hearts of persons of sensibility, an abhorrence and heart-sickening dread of the former, and a love for the latter. Our hearts recoil at the recital of the foregoing slaughter, of but a few short hours; what, then must have been the sanguinary view of the numerous battles, during eight years' hostilities, including the dreadful carnage at Lexington,—the struggle at Yorktown;—and at Bunker Hill! On that once fair rising ground, where the turf looks blackened by fire, yesterday stood a noble mansion; the owner had said in his heart, "Here will I spend the evening of my days, and enjoy the fruits of my labor: my name shall descend with my inheritance, and my children's children shall sport under the trees that I have planted!" But alas! the devastation of an enemy has swept away in a moment, the toil of years; wasted, not enjoyed:—and if he escape with his life, the remaining years of his age are desolate; but far more severe the affliction caused by the shrieks of woe, the cries of anguish, resounding from the roadside, or some miserable shelter, of a dying wife and helpless babes imploring protection! The soothing rites of burial are denied, and human limbs are trodden into the earth by human feet! Such a scene set before our minds, is an unpleasant picture; what then, is the reality? May Heaven preserve us from knowing by experience; and long may America be in reality, the "Land of the Free"—justice be dispensed to all; law sit steady on her throne, and the sword be but her servant.

THE FEMALE WHIG OF '76

Composed by Rosanna Sizer, at the age of sixteen years; at the time Danbury was burnt, at the commencement of the Revolutionary War.

King George the Great Tyrant, as we understand,
Sends over his troops to conquer this land;
But our men are resolved to die in the cause,
Before they submit to be under his laws.

Our brave Liberty men, who stand for their right,
Most honorably they do go forth to fight;
But they are afraid when they are all gone,
There will be none left to raise them bread-corn.

Though they go to war they need not for to fear,
We'll do as much work as though they were here;
For to carry on business, I'll now tell you how,
We women must go out and follow the plough.

We'll plough up the ground and the seed we will sow,
And when it is time then the grass we will mow,
And since that the men are obliged to be gone,
The girls must go out to hoeing the corn.

We will pull all the flax as soon as 'twill do,
For there is need enough of it, there is such a crew
That they are almost naked for the want of clothes,
And there is none to be bought as we suppose.

And when at the time of our harvest comes on,
Then into the fields to reaping we'll run;
We'll reap all the grain and will pick all the corn,
And never give out till our work is all done.

When we have got in the grain then we'll thrash out
    some wheat,
And then make some bread for our soldiers to eat;
And since there is not much rum in the land,
We will have some good cider all ready at hand.

Then we'll go to spinning and spin up the flax,
And make soldiers shirts for to put on their backs;
We'll spin all the wool as fast as we can,
And makes coats and blankets for every man.

Now there is a number of Tories that dwell all around,
A parcel of villains in every town,
They do not deserve to have human respect,
Because that their country's good they reject.

These Tories go creeping and skulking around,
Contriving to ruin both country and town;
Their equals on earth they are not to be found,
'Tis hoped they will soon have a berth under ground.

For we'll work the harder and raise the more flax,
To make halters enough for to stretch all their necks;
We'll spare no pains for to get them all hanged,
For surely they are a great curse on the land.

When they are all hanged then we hope to have peace,
And in a short time that these wars they may cease,
For we see that the force of Great Britain's not much,
For this they have proved by hiring the Dutch.

Now to our brave heroes that have the command,
Hold out with good courage your foes to withstand!
We hope in a short time you will conquer them all,
For the pride of Great Britain must soon have a fall.

THOMAS HERTTELL'S ACCOUNT

For the *Sun*.

NEW YORK, ———, 1832.

Colonel John Fellows:

SIR—In answer to your inquiries in regard to the conduct of the British troops which stormed Fort Griswold, at Groton in Connecticut, during the Revolutionary War, it may be proper to premise, that being at New London at the time of its capture and conflagration by the British forces under the command of that infamous traitor, General Benedict Arnold, on the 6th of September, 1781, I was an eye witness of the attack on Fort Griswold, on the east side of New London harbour. Though a minute detail of all the interesting occurrences connected with that affair may not be necessary to the object of your inquiry, I deem it proper to embrace the present occasion to note, among others, some matters which I have not seen recorded in any history of the war of the Revolution.

That portion of Arnold's forces which invested Fort Griswold was variously stated at a thousand to fifteen hundred men; (the British said eight hundred,) and were commanded by Lieutenant Colonel Eyre. Their incursion, early in the morning, was so sudden and unexpected that only 178 militia (officers included) were enabled to reach the fort, before it became necessary to close the gates. The enemy divided into two columns, made the attack simultaneously on the east and west sides of the fort. That on the east was led on by Lieutenant Colonel Eyre, who fell on the first assault. That on the west was commanded by Major Montgomery, who was killed near the close of the action. Three times did the British columns advance in close order, with trailed arms, and on a run at full speed, with their officers in their rear to oblige them to keep their position, and to goad them on; and three times did they quail before a little band of brave, but disciplined republican soldiers, who caused "death and destruction" in "a lead and iron tempest," exultingly to revel in blood and carnage, through their frittered and flying ranks. Here the conflict seemed to be drawing to a close. The fort ceased firing, and nothing was seen of the enemy but a few officers riding to and fro, endeavoring to rally the scattered fragments of their broken columns. The men, dismayed and disheartened, had taken shelter,— some behind rocks—some in holes—some behind hillocks, and others lay flat, under cover of the undulations of the ground; and none appeared standing within sight and reach from the fort. They had ceased firing, except as if in despair and despite, a single musket was occasionally discharged from the lurking place of a skulking fugitive. A random shot from one of those accidentally cut the halyards of the flagstaff, and the colors were consequently, by a brisk southwest wind, blown outside of the fort. This unfortunate occurrence scarcely gave plausibility to the falsehood immediately proclaimed by the British officers, "that the fort had struck;" or in their polished and more common phrase, "the damn'd Yankees had struck their colors." Thus deceived, and drawn from their hiding places, a fourth attack ensued, and though more irregular, protracted and bloody than either of the preceding, was finally successful. But a dear bought victory it was! The loss of the British was more than double the whole number of Americans who were in the fort!!

Considering the great disparity of the conflicting forces;—a few undisciplined citizens and farmers,—many of whom had never before been in battle, or had never seen a gun fired in anger; engaged with more than four times their own number, of veteran, regular, disciplined troops; a more obstinate, determined, resolute and gallant defence perhaps never before occurred in any nation;—a more protracted, hard fought and bloody battle probably was not fought during our revolutionary struggle; and certainly none which reflected more honor on American bravery, or more dishonor on British troops.

On entering the works the officer, on whom had devolved the command of the remnant of the British forces, demanded, "Who commands this fort?" The gallant Colonel Ledyard, advancing, answered, "Sir, I had the honor once, but now you have!" and presented the hilt of his sword to the victor; who demanded, "Do you know the rules of war?" "Certainly," said Colonel Ledyard. "Then," replied the savage victor, "you Rebel, prepare for death;" and immediately, with Colonel Ledyard's own sword ran him through the body!! A general massacre by the British then ensued, after which seventy or more of the dead and badly wounded of the Americans were collected and laid side by side on their backs, and deliberately and brutally bayoneted again!

One young man, a nephew of Colonel Ledyard, was discovered secreted in the gun-room, covered with wounds; but who saved his life by bribery! Only one man (John Clark, of New London) was killed before the enemy had entered the fort; when the British had lost nearly half of their troops. And only one man of the Americans (and he by stratagem) escaped without a wound. To complete the work of cruelty and death, the remaining wounded Americans, some of whom might have survived, were thrown into waggons and precipitated down the hill on the summit of which the fort is situated, towards the river. Some were instantly killed,—others were badly injured, and but few, if any, survived this act of wanton brutality;—and certainly no individual American who defended the fort and escaped death, was indebted for his life to the magnanimity or humanity of British officers or men. In concurrence with the general and deep indignation excited by the above mentioned cruelties of the enemy, General Washington gave orders to General Wayne to retaliate on the British garrison at Stony Point;—disobedience of which order was overlooked and excused on account of its humanity.[1]

I could add many other interesting details of occurrences which took place on the memorable occasion above noted, and which would honorably contrast the bravery and humanity of American citizen soldiers with the savage brutality of the mercenary myrmidons of the British king, George III. I presume, however, the above is sufficient for the object of your inquiry.

Very respectfully, Yours,

Thos. Herttell.

[1] An error—Stony Point was captured two years before.—(Ed.)